Photographing People

Read *Photographing People* and learn how to—

- Produce successful, effective—and even great—photographs.

- Gain the confidence it takes to put your subject at ease.

- Master the techniques used by professional photographers.

- Develop a photographic style that's distinctly your own.

THE NO NONSENSE LIBRARY

OTHER NO NONSENSE PHOTOGRAPHY GUIDES

Composing Photographs
Photographing Your Vacation
Using Accessory Equipment
Using Creative Techniques
Using Existing Light

OTHER NO NONSENSE GUIDES

Car Guides
Career Guides
Cooking Guides
Financial Guides
Health Guides
Legal Guides
Parenting Guides
Real Estate Guides
Study Guides
Success Guides
Wine Guides

NO NONSENSE PHOTOGRAPHY GUIDE™

PHOTOGRAPHING PEOPLE

A KODAK Book

MICHAEL O'CONNOR

Longmeadow Press

PHOTOGRAPHING PEOPLE

Published by Longmeadow Press, 201 High Ridge Road, Stamford, Connecticut 06904.

ISBN 0-681-40728-X

Produced by The Image Bank in association with Eastman Kodak Company, Rochester, New York.

Kodak is a registered trademark of Eastman Kodak Company and is used under license from Kodak.

The Image Bank® is a registered trademark of The Image Bank, Inc.

Printed in Spain

0 9 8 7 6 5 4 3 2 1

Producer: Solomon M. Skolnick; *Managing Editor:* Elizabeth Loonan; *Editors:* Terri Hardin (The Image Bank), Margaret Buckley (Kodak); *Production Director:* Charles W. Styles (Kodak); *Production Coordinator:* Ann-Louise Lipman (The Image Bank); *Editorial Assistant:* Carol Raguso; *Production Assistant:* Valerie Zars; *Photo Researchers:* Natalie Goldstein, Lenore Weber; *Copy Editor:* Irene S. Korn; *Art Direction and Design:* Chase/Temkin & Associates, Inc.

Cover photographs, left to right: David W. Hamilton, Pamela J. Zilly, David Brownell

For information about the photographs in this book, please contact:
The Image Bank
111 Fifth Avenue
New York, NY 10003

TABLE OF CONTENTS

INTRODUCTION

You probably take more pictures of people than you do of any other subject. But people aren't always easy to photograph well. Are you frequently disappointed by the photos you take? Would you like to get better results and learn how to avoid the most common problems?

Photographing People explains some of the techniques and tricks used by many of the world's top professional photographers when they take pictures of people—tips that you can easily use to your advantage. The illustrations make these tips easy to understand and simple to use.

But taking good photographs of people requires much more than just understanding photographic techniques. The best photographers of people have a skill that isn't easy to teach: being able to work well with people. You must be able to relate to and understand the people you photograph, and sometimes you'll even have to direct your subjects to look or act in a certain way, which isn't always easy to do.

You also need rapid reflexes and responses. You have to recognize a photo opportunity when you see it, and be ready to capture *in an instant* the lines on a face, the twinkle in an eye, or the curve of a lip.

Start by reading this book from beginning to end, and note the areas you find most interesting. Look at the photographs. Which ones appeal most to you, and why? Load your camera and do some experimenting. Try all the techniques to discover what works best for you. If you find terms you don't understand, check the glossary of photographic terms at the back of this book. Terms that are particularly important are in italics in the text and are also listed in the glossary.

Above all, don't feel you have to do everything "by the book." View the ideas, techniques, advice, and photographs in this book as points of departure for your own creativity. Outside of some technical considerations, there really are no hard-and-fast rules in photography. Each situation, each subject, each person, each photographer is unique. That's the challenge and the joy you will discover when you photograph people.

LIGHTING–A KEY TO GREAT PORTRAITS

Michael Going

Understanding light is one of the keys to taking good photographs of any subject, but especially people. There are many types of light and each has distinct qualities and color tone— as well as distinct advantages and drawbacks. Although you may not be able to see all the differences when you are taking the pictures, your film will record them. And you can be sure that when your film is developed, you will see the effect that light has on your pictures.

In Part One, we will discuss exposure: controlling the light that strikes your film. We'll also discuss a number of the most common types of light—strong and hard, diffuse and soft, sunlight, indirect daylight, tungsten light, fluorescent light, and electronic flash. We will go over the differences and offer advice for taking better photographs under various lighting conditions.

CONTROLLING EXPOSURE

Before you start experimenting with different types of light, you may want to know what part light plays in the photographic process.

When film is struck by light, it is *exposed*. The amount of exposure is determined by a combination of two camera controls: *aperture* and *shutter speed*. The more light that strikes your film, the lighter all parts of your photograph will be; less light produces a darker overall picture.

The intensity of the light that strikes the film inside your camera is controlled by the size of the lens opening (called aperture). Apertures are measured in *f*-numbers (or *f-stops*). If you have a camera with manual exposure control, you will see the *f*-numbers marked on your lens. Typical openings for 35 mm camera lenses are *f*/2.8, *f*/4., *f*/5.6, *f*/8, *f*/11, *f*/16, and *f*/22. The higher the number, the smaller the aperture will be; smaller apertures admit less light. For example, *f*/11 admits less light than *f*/8.

Your camera shutter controls the length of time that light is allowed to act on the film. The shutter speeds most often used are fractions of a second, such as 1/60, 1/125, and 1/250, but they

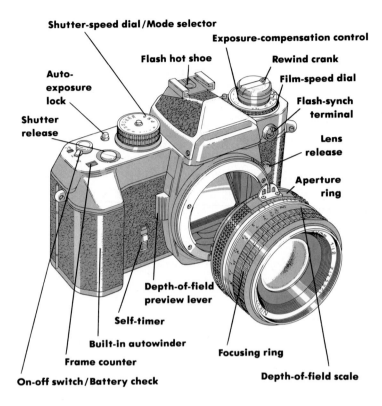

Shutter-speed dial/Mode selector

Exposure-compensation control

Flash hot shoe

Rewind crank

Auto-exposure lock

Film-speed dial

Flash-synch terminal

Shutter release

Lens release

Aperture ring

Depth-of-field preview lever

Self-timer

Built-in autowinder

Focusing ring

Frame counter

On-off switch/Battery check

Depth-of-field scale

are listed on the camera shutter-speed dial as 60, 125, 250, and so on. If you have an adjustable camera, you can manually set shutter speeds. However, if your camera is partially or fully automatic, you will have limited—or no—control over the shutter speed.

Changing either aperture or shutter speed by one stop (by moving to the next number in the series) either doubles the exposure or cuts it in half. For example, $f/8$ admits twice as much light as $f/11$, but only half as much light as $f/5.6$. A shutter speed of 1/60 second allows twice as much light to reach the film as a speed of 1/125 second.

Each time you change the exposure by one stop, you halve or

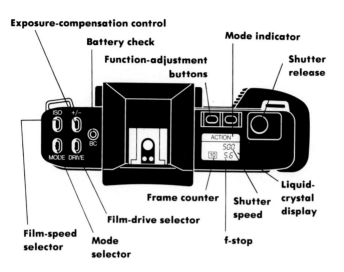

Exposure-compensation control
Battery check
Function-adjustment buttons
Mode indicator
Shutter release

ISO +/−
MODE DRIVE
BC

ACTION
500
10 5.6

Frame counter
Shutter speed
Liquid-crystal display
Film-drive selector
f-stop
Film-speed selector
Mode selector

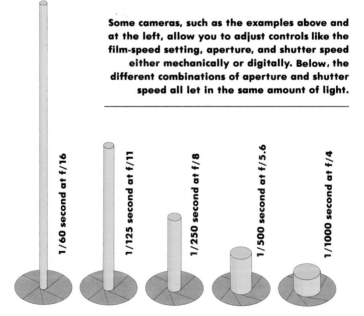

Some cameras, such as the examples above and at the left, allow you to adjust controls like the film-speed setting, aperture, and shutter speed either mechanically or digitally. Below, the different combinations of aperture and shutter speed all let in the same amount of light.

1/60 second at f/16

1/125 second at f/11

1/250 second at f/8

1/500 second at f/5.6

1/1000 second at f/4

double the exposure. Changing by two stops means that either four times or one-quarter as much light acts on the film.

If you change both aperture and shutter speed the same number of stops in opposite directions, your exposure will remain the same. However, other factors—such as *depth of field* (which is controlled by aperture) or the ability to *stop motion* (which is controlled by shutter speed)—change. This provides you with a great deal of creative control over how your pictures look.

The following chart gives suggested exposures for some common daylight situations. Use these settings as a guide. Bracket your exposure by at least plus and minus one stop for especially important pictures.

SUGGESTED DAYLIGHT EXPOSURES

LIGHTING	ISO 100	ISO 200	ISO 400	ISO 1000	ISO 1600
Bright or hazy sun on sand or snow	f/16 1/250	f/16 1/500	f/16 1/1000	f/22 1/1000	f/22 1/2000
Bright or hazy sun (distinct shadows)	f/16 1/125	f/16 1/250	f/16 1/500	f/16 1/1000	f/22 1/1000
Weak, hazy sun (soft shadows)	f/11 1/125	f/11 1/250	f/11 1/500	f/11 1/1000	f/16 1/1000
Cloudy-bright (no shadows)	f/8 1/125	f/8 1/250	f/8 1/500	f/8 1/1000	f/11 1/1000
Open shade or heavy overcast	f/5.6 1/125	f/5.6 1/250	f/5.6 1/500	f/5.6 1/1000	f/8 1/1000

Note: With ISO 64 film, increase the exposures suggested for ISO 100 film by one stop, i.e., use the next larger lens opening or the next slower shutter speed.

OUTDOORS IN DIRECT SUNLIGHT

Although it seems ideal for picture-taking and looks beautiful, bright sunlight frequently causes problems when you take pictures of people. Bright sunlight is extremely harsh and can produce unwanted contrast. For instance, shadow areas in pictures can appear completely black, while the brightest areas are too light to show any detail.

How much contrast you get depends on when and where you take the picture. If it's during the middle of the day (with the sun almost directly overhead), your photograph will show unflattering shadows under eyebrows, noses, and chins. Sometimes the shadows will be deep and dark enough to hide the eyes completely and conceal facial expressions.

But when you take photographs at the beach (or in any setting with a large white surface below the subject), the sand reflects a great deal of light. In the middle of the day, sand will

In direct sunlight, colors can be warm and strong. The angle of the sun, however, can be uncomfortable for your subject, and creates deep shadows with very little detail.

Paul Slaughter

At the beach, sand and water reflect a great deal of sunlight. Although this family is under the beach umbrella, the sand reflects enough light to fill what could have been deep shadows.

Inone/Grimberg

bounce overhead sunlight back onto your subject from below. When this reflected light is enough to soften and "fill" shadows, pictures can come out beautifully.

Be careful! If your camera or exposure meter reads the bright light reflecting from the sand, it can underexpose the scene. Then the sand will look gray and your subject will be too dark. That's why, whenever possible, you should take an exposure-meter reading directly from your subject's face. Here's how:

MAKING A CLOSE-UP METER READING

1. Get close to your subject so that his or her face fills most of the frame.
2. Take a reading with your camera's built-in meter or a separate hand-held meter.
3. Move back to include more background, but take the picture at the exposure setting determined by your close-up reading.

PHOTOGRAPHING PEOPLE

Although the horse and rider above are backlit by the low morning sun, the fine mist reflects and diffuses the light to create soft, even lighting and give the photograph a romantic aura. The backlighting in the photograph at the right is much more obvious. The golfer is silhouetted by low afternoon sun in a clear sky. There is no reflected light to fill in his features, and the shadows are deep and long.

You have probably heard that the proper way to take a picture outdoors is to have the sun shining over your shoulder from behind you. And if you have done this, you probably have many pictures of your family and friends squinting into the camera or casting their faces in shadow by holding their hands above their eyes.

Why not try turning your subjects around so that the sun is behind them? This technique is called *backlighting*. It can be flattering, but exposure can be tricky because most cameras read the brightness of an overall scene. If your subject's face is in the shade and is a relatively small part of the entire scene, your camera will probably expose for the brighter background and the face will be too dark.

If your camera has a backlight (exposure-compensation) control, read your camera manual so that you can use it properly If your camera doesn't have this control, follow the steps (on page 14) to make a close-up meter reading of your subject's face.

If your camera has manual exposure control, you can also compensate by following this guideline: The proper exposure for the face of a backlit subject is normally one to two stops more than the exposure for the overall scene (as indicated by the camera meter). Increase the aperture (or use a slower shutter speed) to increase exposure by 1, 1 1/2, and 2 stops, and then study the results. With a little experience, you will be able to judge the proper compensation automatically.

Finally, you can use *fill-in flash* (see page 33) or reflectors (see page 22) to add light to a face in shadow.

SHADE AND OVERCAST DAYS

If sunlight is extremely strong and no reflective surfaces are available, why not move your subject out of the direct sunlight and into the shade—under a ledge or an awning, or on the shadowed side of a building? On a bright day, there is plenty of light in the shade to illuminate your subject. This way you will avoid excessive contrast, and your subject will be more comfortable.

PHOTOGRAPHING PEOPLE

Nancy Brown

A yellow tarp provides shelter from a summer rain shower and casts a sunny glow on the family above. Take a meter reading directly from the subject in situations like these, and remember that a colored awning may tint your subjects. The photograph at the right shows the soft, even effect of fill light. This man was photographed in the shade close to a beach, where the sand, water, and cloudless sky reflected a good deal of light.

Walter Meeker

Be aware, however, that shade also causes some photographic problems. The light under colored awnings made of thin material may have the distinct color cast of the awning; also, the shade under trees is often distinctly green, and green makes skin tones less attractive. These color casts will be obvious when you know to look out for them. If you run into any of them, move your subject into a shaded area that does not appear to have a color cast.

When you photograph a person in the shade on a bright day, you also need to be careful about your exposure. Make sure the shady area fills the entire viewfinder frame; even the slightest bit of bright, direct sunlight can produce incorrect exposure. Then the shady area that includes your subject will be underexposed, and your subject might even be unrecognizable. If you are unsure about your exposure-meter reading, you can safeguard yourself by increasing your exposure by one stop.

Also look out for problem backgrounds. In many shady settings, the background will be close behind your subject, and a cluttered background or cracked wall can be a distraction.

Ted Kawalerski

If you want to isolate your subjects from the elements around them, use a wide aperture and focus on their eyes. This will keep your subjects sharp while throwing the background out of focus.

PHOTOGRAPHING PEOPLE

The soft, even light of an overcast day can make bright colors really stand out, and it's equally flattering to pastels and flesh tones.

It's easy to subdue a difficult background if you can control your aperture manually. Just make the background go out of focus by using a large lens aperture, such as $f/2.8$ or $f/3.5$. Have your subject move as far from a wall or cluttered background as possible while still remaining in the shade. Make sure his or her eyes are in focus. If you are using an automatic camera and aren't able to control your lens aperture manually, it might be best to look for another location.

Why feel you have to put your camera away when the sky is cloudy? Soft, diffused light is usually more flattering to faces than bright, direct sunlight. The light on an overcast day may seem gray and dim, but it is even, does not cast harsh shadows, and provides ideal opportunities for photographs of people.

Colors can be beautiful on an overcast day in a way that they are not on a bright day. The even light coming through thin clouds is ideal for showing soft colors and pastels to best advantage. The light on an overcast day is slightly "bluer" than direct sunlight, which contrasts with bright reds and yellows, making them jump out with vibrancy. (For an explanation of *color temperature,* see page 23.)

DAYLIGHT INDOORS

The location and size of a window obviously determine what kind of light and how much light the window lets in. A large window facing the open north sky provides the softest and most diffuse light, which is wonderful for portraits. A small window admits light that appears to come from a single direction; it casts more distinct shadows than light entering a large window. By the heightened contrast it provides, this type of light gives you the opportunity to make more dramatic statements.

Direct sunlight streaming through a window into a large room, or a room with dark walls and carpets, can cause exposure problems. In situations like this, you must choose whether to expose for the shadow areas or the sunlit areas.

PHOTOGRAPHING PEOPLE

In the photograph above, a large window provides the light. The white walls of the room reflect the light, helping to fill shadows and create even lighting on the subject. The strong directional light in the photograph at the right is not reflected back onto the subject, and gives the image a very dramatic style.

LIGHTING

You can try making the light more even by diffusing it. Fasten tracing paper (or a sheet of thin, translucent white cloth) over the entire window. This will cut down on the amount of light and reduce the contrast.

With any type of window light, many photographers add some fill light to the shadow side of the subject. You can do this by placing a reflector opposite the window, just outside the frame of your viewfinder. This generally produces the most natural effect.

As long as it is white or silver, any good-size, highly reflective surface—a large piece of paper, art board, or even a bed sheet—will produce neutral fill light. Use a colored reflector if you want to tint the reflected light.

The closer the reflector is to your subject, the stronger the effect will be; and the larger the reflective surface, the smoother and softer the fill light will appear on the subject. The angle and height of the reflector also determine how much fill light it provides, as well as what part of the subject the light strikes most directly. If you experiment with the placement and angle of the reflector, make sure you return to your original position after adjusting it or you may not be able to see the difference.

Candlelight	Light Bulbs		Sunrise	Photolamp
1800 K	75 Watt	2820 K	Sunset	3400 K
	100 Watt	2900 K	3000-3100 K	
	200 Watt	2980 K		

PHOTOGRAPHING PEOPLE

TUNGSTEN LIGHT INDOORS

The light from your household lamps—called tungsten light—has a yellow-orange tint. Technically, the color of a light source is called color temperature, which is measured in *degrees Kelvin* (K).

Color temperature ranges from 1800 K to 18000 K. Daylight at noon has a color temperature of about 5500 K; tungsten lamps, used in photography, are approximately 3200 K.

The most common type of film is *daylight film*. For example, KODACOLOR GOLD Films and KODAK EKTAR Films for color prints are balanced for exposure to daylight. KODAK EKTACHROME 100 HC, 200, and 400 Films, and films such as KODACHROME 25, 64, and 200, which produce color slides, are all balanced for exposure to daylight. When you use these films with the sun as your light source, the colors in your pictures will be properly balanced. But if you use daylight film under tungsten light, its warm, orange tint will be more obvious to the film than it is to your eyes when you take the picture. Sometimes you might choose to use a daylight film in tungsten light to create a warm, intimate effect.

Jim Ludtke

| Daylight
5500 K | Overcast Sky
7000 K | Open Shade
12000-18000 K |

Electronic Flash
5500-6000 K

An important note: Matching the film to the light source is not nearly as critical with films for color prints as it is with color-slide films. KODACOLOR GOLD and EKTAR Films produce negatives, which are then printed on photographic paper. During the printing step, it is possible to make corrections that will produce more accurate color balance in the prints. But when you use color-slide film, the film you expose in your camera is the same film that's returned to you as mounted slides. No printing step is involved. Therefore, it's more important to choose a color-slide film that's balanced for the type of illumination in the scenes you photograph.

If you don't want an orange tint in color slides of scenes with tungsten light, KODAK EKTACHROME 160 Film (Tungsten) is an excellent film choice. Its speed of ISO 160 is fast enough for many moderately low light situations. And if you want to use the same film outdoors in daylight, you can expose it at ISO 100 with a No. 85B filter.

Erik Leigh Simmons

This photograph, taken on daylight film with available room light, required a slow shutter speed and wide aperture. The photographer used a tripod to steady his camera. Note the warm, orange cast of the light from the tungsten desk lamp, and the private, intimate feeling created by the small pool of light.

KODAK Film	For use with*	Film Speed and Filter		
		Daylight	Tungsten Lamps (3200 K)	Photolamps (3400 K)
KODACHROME 25 (slide)	DEF	25 None	6 No. 80A	8 No. 80B
KODACHROME 64 (slide)	DEF	64 None	16 No. 80A	20 No. 80B
KODACHROME 200 (slide)	DEF	200 None	50 No. 80A	64 No. 80B
KODACHROME 40 (slide)	P	25 No. 85	32 No. 82A	40 None
EKTACHROME 100 HC (slide)	DEF	100 None	25 No. 80A	32 No. 80B
EKTACHROME 200 (slide)	DEF	200 None	50 No. 80A	64 No. 80B
EKTACHROME 400 (slide)	DEF	400 None	100 No. 80A	125 No. 80B
EKTACHROME 160 (slide)	T	100 No. 85B	160 None	125 No. 81A
KODACOLOR GOLD 100 (print)	DEF	100 None	25 No. 80A	32 No. 80B
KODACOLOR GOLD 200 (print)	DEF	200 None	50 No. 80A	64 No. 80B
KODACOLOR GOLD 400 (print)	DEF	400 None	100 No. 80A	125 No. 80B
KODACOLOR GOLD 1600 (print)	DEF	1600 None	400 No. 80A	500 No. 80B
EKTAR 25 (print)	DEF	25 None	6 No. 80A	8 No. 80B
EKTAR 125 (print)	DEF	125 None	32 No. 80A	40 No. 80B
EKTAR 1000 (print)	DEF	1000 None	250 No. 80A	320 No. 80B

*DEF—Balanced for daylight or electronic flash.
  T—Balanced for tungsten lamps or existing tungsten light
  P—Balanced for photolamps.

You can also use a No. 80A filter to balance the color temperature of light from tungsten lamps to daylight films. But because this filter absorbs quite a bit of light and reduces the amount of light that reaches the film, you will have to increase exposure by two stops. Unless you are using a very fast film, you may not have enough film speed for many situations.

Most cameras with through-the-lens meters will automatically compensate for the filter. Your choice of film and filters depends on what you want your photographs to "say," what kind of atmosphere or mood you want them to have. There is no "right"

Tim Bieber, Inc.

This photograph, made on daylight film, shows the difference in color between daylight and tungsten light. Photographed just after sunset, the outside of the house is illuminated by light from the open sky, and the inside is illuminated by tungsten household lamps.

or "wrong" other than what is appropriate to the subject, and even that is largely a matter of taste.

Choose a fast film (usually ISO 400 or above), because the light level will be relatively low. Place your camera on a tripod or other camera support when you use shutter speeds slower than 1/30 second.

MIXED LIGHTING

Pools of color from various light sources can give you dramatic, effective pictures. The most common combination of light sources is a mixture of daylight and tungsten light (household lamps). Tungsten lights have a noticeably warmer cast than daylight, although rays from a setting sun can also appear very warm. Like sunsets, tungsten lights add a golden glow to the areas they illuminate. (See pages 22–23 for the exact temperature of tungsten lights.)

In general, you should use a film that is balanced for the predominant light source in the scene. When in doubt, choose a daylight film that's fast enough for low-light conditions, such as KODACOLOR GOLD 400 or 1600 Film for prints, or KODAK EKTACHROME 400 Film for slides. The tungsten light will appear yellow and warm, which will make an appealing photograph.

Another form of mixed lighting—one that is often used by professional photographers—is a combination of tungsten light and electronic flash. For example, a fashion photographer using a daylight film might illuminate the blonde hair of a model with a tungsten spotlight to make it appear gold, and light her face with flash for accurate skin tones.

When you take existing-light pictures in rooms lit by household tungsten lamps, only the areas near the lamps may show up in the pictures. By using *bounce flash*, you can reveal more of the scene, yet maintain a natural look. Here's how:

USING BOUNCE FLASH IN TUNGSTEN LIGHT

1. Position yourself to take a bounce-flash picture. (See page 32 for details on bounce-flash techniques.) Determine the distance from the flash to the bounce surface to the subject.
2. On the flash calculator dial, find the aperture that corresponds to this distance. Set the lens to the aperture one stop larger. For example, if the indicated aperture is $f/8$, set the lens at $f/5.6$.
3. Set the shutter speed to provide correct exposure for the existing tungsten light. Be sure to use a shutter speed of 1/60 second or slower. Mount the camera on a tripod if you use a shutter speed slower than 1/30 second.
4. Set the flash on automatic or manual (don't use it in a dedicated mode). Turn on the flash and aim it at the bounce surface.
5. Take the picture. The light from the flash will provide one-half to one stop less light than the existing light.

FLUORESCENT LIGHT

The effects of fluorescent light on film can vary widely, because there are so many different types of fluorescent tubes in use. In general, fluorescent light imparts a green or blue-green cast. Although you can use filters such as an FLD filter (to balance daylight film to fluorescent light) and an FLT filter (to balance tungsten film to fluorescent light), results are unpredictable. When you can't avoid fluorescent light, use a daylight-type color print film so that some correction can be made during printing.

USING FLASH

A battery-powered electronic flash is probably the most portable and popular means of providing enough light for pictures of people indoors or outdoors at night. Flash units emit light for only a brief instant (approximately 1/2000 second), so they can freeze most motion. (You'll find this especially useful in a rapidly changing situation, such as a party.) It's easy to get a clear picture.

Use daylight film with electronic flash. The color temperature of the flash is close to that of daylight. If you use tungsten-balanced film, your pictures will be extremely blue.

Flash equipment. Many modern cameras have a built-in flash unit, and all you need to do is turn it on or pop it up. Some cameras even turn on the flash automatically whenever the meter determines that the scene is too dark for proper exposure without flash. These built-in units usually have less power than separate accessory units, and are not useful for large scenes or for subjects more than 10 to 15 feet from the camera (although flash ranges for some built-in units may be considerably greater with high-speed film).

If you want to invest in a detachable, portable flash unit, you can choose from two general types. The easiest for a beginner is an automatic flash, the more modern type of unit. It has a

PHOTOGRAPHING PEOPLE

You can mount detachable flash units directly on your camera, or connect them with a flash-sync (synchronization) cord and hand-hold them for different effects. As a general rule, the larger the flash unit, the more powerful it is.

sensor that measures light bouncing back from a scene, and it automatically shuts off when it has emitted the proper amount of light. The most advanced type of automatic flash unit, called *dedicated,* is designed for specific brands or models of cameras. It sets the proper *flash-synchronization shutter speed,* measures the amount of flash illumination, and exchanges information with the camera to provide proper exposure. Most automatic units are not quite so advanced, and have two or more automatic settings or modes, in addition to a manual setting.

The other type of unit is a manual design that delivers the same amount of light each time the flash fires. It is usually less expensive than an automatic unit, but you must control exposure by adjusting the camera aperture or by changing the distance from the flash to the subject.

Using automatic and manual flash. Whatever type of flash you use, you have to use it properly to get the kind of picture you want. See the following step-by-step procedures for manual and automatic flash units.

USING FLASH

1. Set your camera shutter at the proper flash-synchronization (sync) speed, which is usually indicated on the shutter-speed dial (usually 1/60 or 1/125 second). See your flash manual. FOR AUTOMATIC: Set the flash at the speed (ISO) of the film you are using.

2. Determine the distance to your subject (you can use the focusing ring on your lens to help).

3. Set the flash to the automatic setting indicated on the calculator dial for the range that includes the distance you determined in Step 2. FOR MANUAL: Set your lens aperture at the *f*-stop indicated on the flash calculator dial for that subject distance.

4. Fire away!

FLASH TECHNIQUES

You can use many simple, common-sense techniques for producing pleasing effects in your photographs. Here are some that will help you be more creative, competent, and comfortable when you take flash pictures.

Off-camera flash. You can produce a flattering, classic, three-quarters lighting effect (see page 49) by placing your flash off to one side and slightly higher than the camera. Try holding the flash in your hand with your arm extended, or mount it on a tripod (or other support) next to you. An inexpensive accessory extension sync cord will allow you to do this.

With automatic, detachable flash units, the accessory extension sync cord allows the sensor to remain mounted on the camera, facing the subject. This makes proper exposure easy—the equipment does everything automatically. If you have a manual flash unit, base your exposure on the flash-to-subject distance rather than on the camera-to-subject distance.

PHOTOGRAPHING PEOPLE

This photograph was taken with an off-camera flash held above and to the right of the camera. This method provides more texture and three-dimensional modeling of the subject's skin and hair, and prevents reflections in the man's eyeglasses.

To use off-camera bounce flash, aim a detachable flash unit at a wall or reflector. The flash-sync cord connects the camera to the flash unit so that the shutter and flash both operate at the same time. The flash will freeze any movement.

When bouncing the light from your flash off the ceiling or wall, be sure the angle is correct. If your aim is off, the light will fall in front of or behind your subject.

Bounce flash. To provide more even illumination over a large area and to soften and fill in shadows, many professional photographers use a technique known as bounce flash.

It's simple. Rather than firing your flash directly at the subject, you "bounce" it off a large reflecting surface, such as a low white ceiling or a nearby white wall. Light bounced from a ceiling is like sunlight or light from an overhead room lamp, and light bounced off a wall often looks as if it came through a large window. But be careful about the surface you use as a reflector; any color in the reflector will tint your photograph.

Many modern automatic flash units allow you to tilt the flashtube and reflector while the flash sensor remains facing the subject and reads the light reflected from the subject. This makes exposure easy. Rely on the sensor, but be sure to set your flash range for the longer distance (flash-to-reflector plus reflector-to-subject) that the light will actually travel.

There is an important point to remember with bounce flash. The actual flash-to-subject distance is much greater than the distance from the camera to the subject. The light from the flash has to travel to the reflective surface and then to the subject. Also keep in mind that the reflecting surface will absorb some of the light, so you might have to increase exposure.

With a manual flash unit, add the distance from the flash to the reflector to the distance from the reflector to the subject to determine the total flash-to-subject distance. Compensating for the light absorbed by the reflecting surface is more difficult; a good rule of thumb is to increase exposure by one or two stops for normal white walls.

Be sure that the reflected light illuminates the scene the way you want. Too sharp an angle may cause the light to fall short of your subject; too great an angle can cast the light behind your subject.

Fill-in flash. You can produce flattering portraits outdoors by supplementing the existing sunlight with electronic flash. This technique is known as fill-in flash—the light from the flash is used to fill (lighten) shadows created by the sun. It is particularly useful with backlit subjects when you want to capture detail in a backlit face as well as in the background.

Don't overpower the existing light—the point is to create a natural effect. Don't use too much fill and make the flash look

These photographs show the dramatic difference fill-in flash can make. The light source is behind the woman, and the exposure was based on the general lighting conditions. In the photograph at top, the woman's face is a bit dark. The added flash in the image below fills in the shadows and separates the subject from the background. To decrease depth of field and further isolate a subject from a busy background, use a wide aperture.

PHOTOGRAPHING PEOPLE

obvious; use just enough to fill the shadows. Here's a rule of thumb: Use about half as much power as it would take to illuminate the scene entirely by flash. Often, you'll need even less power.

Many electronic flash units have a variable power control, which makes it easy to turn down the output of the flash. You can also "trick" many automatic units into providing less power by setting the film speed (ISO) dial at a speed higher than the speed of the film you are using. Doubling the film speed will cut the power in half (by one stop). You can cut the effective power of any flash by covering the flashtube and reflector with a piece of translucent white cloth or paper, but you'll have to make tests to determine exactly how much the covering reduces the light.

If necessary, you can turn an automatic flash into a manual flash even if it doesn't have a manual setting. Just block the sensor with a piece of dark tape and the flash will fire at full power every time.

USING FILL-IN FLASH

1. Set your camera at the proper flash-sync shutter speed (usually 1/60 or 1/125 second).
2. Make a meter reading of an important sunlit area, and set the aperture to give correct exposure of that area.
3. On the flash calculator dial, find the distance that corresponds to an aperture one stop larger than the aperture you set in step 2. For example, if you set the aperture at *f*/11, find the distance that corresponds to *f*/8. Stand at this distance from your subject to take the picture. (Use a zoom lens if you want to adjust the image size.)
4. Set the flash on manual, or cover the sensor on an automatic flash unit.
5. Take the picture.

AVOIDING FLASH PROBLEMS

Here are some of the more common problems, as well as some basic techniques that will allow you to avoid mistakes and get the most from your flash.

Problem #1: *A black strip covering part of the image.* This means your camera was probably set at a shutter speed faster than the proper sync speed. Your camera shutter must be fully open when the flash fires, or only a section of the frame will be exposed. The proper sync speed should be indicated on the shutter-speed dial. With most cameras, speeds slower than the proper sync speed (1/60 or 1/125 second) will also work.

Problem #2: *Unwanted reflections.* Avoid mirrors or windows behind your subject; they are likely to reflect the light from the flash and produce an unpleasant hot spot (bright reflection) in your picture. Or worse: the reflection can be bright enough to fool the flash sensor and cause underexposure.

Also, any light-colored surface—whether it's a large white wall, or a shiny or light-colored object in the foreground between you and your subject—can fool the sensor into underexposing your subject. The flash sensor may read the light reflected from that object and leave your main subject too dark.

You can avoid problems by eliminating foreground objects, or you can use a manual setting to override the sensor.

Similarly, trying to photograph your subject standing next to a glass case that holds an item of interest simply won't work. You are likely to capture only the reflection of your flash in the glass, obscuring the item inside and underexposing your subject.

Problem #3: *Red-eye.* This distressing occurrence is a reflection of your flash from blood vessels in the back of the eye. To prevent this from happening, you can try turning on all the lights in the rooms, or you can try the bounce-flash technique (see page 32).

PHOTOGRAPHING PEOPLE

Melchior DiGiacomo

Red-eye is a common problem in flash photos taken in relatively dim light.

One last tip for using flash units: Always carry extra batteries for your flash unit. Prolong the life of your batteries by removing them from your unit if you're not going to use it for a week or so; also, removing batteries will prevent them from leaking acid onto your equipment and damaging it.

PART TWO

PHOTOGRAPHING GROUPS AND INDIVIDUALS

André Gallant

The difference between photographing a group and photographing an individual involves more than just the number of people in the picture.

The most important thing in making a group portrait, for example, is establishing unity between the group members. Sometimes this can be as easy as having a football team pose in uniform. But while you can photograph groups in a variety of different ways, it is the dynamics of the group members together that carries the picture.

In a portrait of a single person—be it a man, woman, or child—the relationship of the individual to his or her surroundings is much more important. That's why portraits of individuals are more likely to challenge your creativity.

In Part Two, we will discuss how to pose people for portraits—how to establish contact and unity in groups, and how to establish a relationship between an individual and his or her environment. You'll learn how to set up your own portrait studio. You'll even learn how to relax your subjects (and yourself), charm expressions out of them, and take flattering photos that will keep them coming back for more!

GROUPS

When photographing large groups, it's often hard to show everyone clearly. You can overcome this problem by posing the group in a setting that places group members on various visual levels naturally—for example, on a hillside (outdoors) or on a staircase (indoors). This not only makes it easier to show each person, regardless of height, but also adds interest to your portrait.

The classic pose for groups is to arrange their faces and bodies to form a circle. It is frequently used by many professional photographers. In fact, this technique is so common that most groups of people being photographed don't even need to be told to form a circle; they just do it instinctively!

Arranging a large group on different levels creates an interesting arrangement and keeps all the people in focus. When you work with a group as large as the one above, check your viewfinder frame to be sure that everyone is included before snapping the picture; take a step back if necessary. The portraits at the left and opposite illustrate placement on different levels, physical contact, and getting your subjects to relax.

PHOTOGRAPHING PEOPLE

This pose leads the viewer's eye smoothly from one person to another. Sometimes, however, the circular motion is less obvious than faces forming a circle; it could be as subtle as an arm curving around someone else's shoulders or waist.

When you do not pose a group tightly, encourage your subjects to form a loose arrangement with some interest and difference in their positions. Encourage some to kneel or sit

Bil Plummer

You can show unity between the people in your photographs in different ways. In the image above, the baseball team poses tightly together; their uniforms provide bright color and link the subjects. In the bottom photograph, the arms of grandfather and grandson are compositionally unifying, as well as emotionally moving.

PHOTOGRAPHING PEOPLE

while others stand—nothing is worse than a group of people standing stiffly shoulder-to-shoulder, staring at the camera.

Another way to create a feeling of unity is to arrange subjects around an object of which they are obviously proud, and to which they all relate. Take the family pet, for example. A cat or dog in the center of the group will pull the people together and add a focal point visually. Or you might pose a group of firefighters around their firetruck. Even if the firefighters are out of uniform, the truck will provide a link between them.

Physical contact also conveys a feeling of unity. Have one person put his or her arms around the shoulders of two others, or have someone rest a hand on the arm of someone else. This establishes not only a physical link, but a visual link as well.

One problem you may encounter when you photograph a large group of people in relatively low light is shallow *depth of field*. You must have enough depth of field in the picture for

Tim Bieber, Inc.

Photographing several people indoors in low light can create a depth-of-field problem. If you want all your subjects to be in sharp focus, you may have to position them all at the same distance from the camera.

everyone's face to be in focus. You can avoid this problem by positioning each person approximately the same distance from the camera. This way, the shallow depth of field will be less obvious, and everyone's face will be sharp. (For more on depth of field, see the glossary, page 78.)

You may want to try the *bounce-flash* technique described on page 32. This technique works very well with groups because the light falls more evenly over a large area. The result is usually more flattering.

If you are working with a built-in flash, it is a good idea to position each of your subjects at about the same distance from the camera. If you don't, the flash may provide too little light for the people farthest from you. Many built-in flash units have too little power to penetrate deeply shadowed areas; and since exposure is almost always based on the nearest subject, a person a few feet in front of the rest of the group can make the others virtually disappear into shadow.

Finally, you've got your group exactly where you want them, and you are about to capture them on film. Telling them to say cheese may be the classic method for getting smiles from all your subjects at the same time, but who says it's the best? Here's a 3-step method for getting more photogenic expressions from a group:

GETTING GOOD EXPRESSIONS

1. Encourage your subjects to relax. Have them talk to each other; this creates a much more realistic and casual situation.
2. Retain enough control over the situation so that when it's time to take pictures, you will have their complete attention.
3. Take a number of pictures to help ensure that you get at least one shot with good expressions from everyone.

PHOTOGRAPHING PEOPLE

It may take your subjects a few minutes to relax and warm up to the camera. Take the time to make a few extra shots; your subjects will probably lose that stiff, posed look.

INDIVIDUALS

When you photograph an individual, it is important to talk to your subject as you work. Say how good you think your model looks, and how good the pictures will be. Making your subject feel right about his or her appearance is a key to good photographs. It's no accident that many professional fashion photographers keep up an almost constant banter on the set. Even professional models like to be told how good-looking they are.

David W. Hamilton

The subject's confidence in the photographer is clear in this image. The golden quality of the late-afternoon light and the subject's pose and friendly expression combine to make this a successful portrait.

Talking to your subject also helps you to be as secure and confident in your role as photographer as your subject must be in the role of model. It establishes a rapport between you and your subject that translates into better photographs.

Concentrate on your subject's eyes, and try to capture their essence. In *all* portraits, eyes are the most important feature. In a good photograph, they reveal the subject's personality.

A common and very effective technique is to have your subject look straight at the camera. Direct eye contact produces a feeling of immediacy and intimacy.

Sometimes your subject may be looking off to the side of the frame, or at something in the picture, such as a piano keyboard. Although these poses may seem different—more contemplative—it is still important for you to concentrate on the eyes: they will tell the story of your portrait.

A feeling of intimacy is created by tight cropping and direct eye contact. A telephoto (135 mm) lens was used for this portrait, allowing enough distance between the camera and subject for him to feel relaxed.

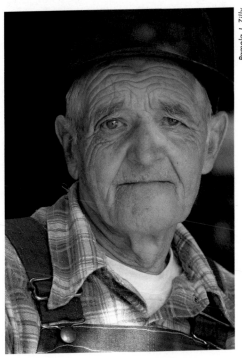

Pamela J. Zilly

For this quiet and contemplative shot of a young woman, the photographer used a wide aperture to create very shallow depth of field. The facial features are sharp, while neck and shoulders are blurred.

When you are photographing in low light with a large lens aperture (which means shallow depth of field) you must focus on the subject's eyes to make sure all the facial features are sharp.

Eyeglasses can cause problems because they reflect light. If your subject wears eyeglasses, let him or her keep them on. To avoid reflections, tilt your subject's head either slightly forward or to the side.

The setting for a portrait can make a great deal of difference in how a picture presents a person. The surroundings should not only say something about your subject, but should also be reassuring, so that he or she feels relaxed. It's a good idea to stay away from noisy or busy locations. A quiet, secluded area allows both photographer and subject to concentrate on making pictures without distraction.

If you are very concerned about distractions, why not create your own portrait studio? Setting up a portrait studio (or location) is easy; all you really need is a large, diffuse light source, a neutral background, a reflector, and perhaps a few props.

This subject would not feel as comfortable as he appears in this portrait if he had removed his eyeglasses. Simply tilting the subject's head forward avoided the problem of flash reflections.

David W. Hamilton

The classic *existing-light* photography studio is a medium-size room with white walls, a light-colored floor, and a large window facing the open sky. The sky provides the light, and the white floors and walls (if they are close enough to the subject) reflect fill light into the shadow areas.

If the walls are too far away to reflect enough light, prop a large white board opposite the window, as close to your subject as necessary to provide enough light.

In your studio, you might practice *three-quarters lighting,* which can help make very flattering portraits. This is a lighting angle achieved by positioning your subject at about a 45-degree angle to the window, while you (and your camera) are between the subject and the window.

Studios—and studio situations—can get much more complicated, but it's always a good idea to keep things as simple as possible. That way, you'll be able to concentrate on your subject's pose and expression without being distracted, and achieve great results.

_____**49**

INDIVIDUALS

ADULTS

When you photograph a group, the presence of other adults is both relaxing and reassuring. No one feels alone when there is someone else with whom to talk, or even joke.

Photographing adults as individuals, however, is more difficult. Grown men and women tend to be self-conscious and nervous about looking good. To put your subject at ease, review the steps for photographing individuals on pages 46–49.

Before you begin, take a moment to familiarize yourself with your subject's best (and worst) features. With this information—and a few tricks—you can make your subject look his or her best.

For example, suppose that your subject is partially or completely bald. The top of his head may be oily and this oiliness will reflect light and create a hot spot. Blot the subject's forehead with a tissue before photographing; if necessary, apply pancake makeup that contains corn silk.

You can improve a too-long nose with the right camera angle and lighting. Photograph straight-on at face level (no higher) or slightly below, and direct the light onto the front of the subject's face. This lighting angle, called *frontlighting*, will flatten the features to a uniform proportion. If your subject's lips are attractive, have your subject moisten them before you shoot to create an exciting image. Also try shooting your subject's eyes—often the most attractive feature—at various angles to create different impressions.

When you photograph a little girl wearing makeup, you'll often get a whimsical, playful picture. However, grown women who wear makeup often want to look "natural" in it. A photograph in which her makeup is obvious can be embarrassing to your subject. If she is wearing heavy makeup, photograph her in soft light. Put a tissue around the light source to diffuse it. (With men, soft light will diminish a "five-o'clock shadow.")

Adults are large; you have to decide how much of them you want to include in the picture. Head and shoulders, half-torso,

PHOTOGRAPHING PEOPLE

Use lighting to your advantage when you photograph the people in your life. Frontlighting, like that used in the image at the right, can flatten features and erase "flaws," but watch out for shiny reflections on the skin. Diffuse lighting, as pictured below, is very flattering and softens makeup.

David W. Hamilton

Don Klumpp

and full figure all require decisions from you: do you shoot up close, or back away and kneel? Look at all these options before you snap the picture. Every situation needs your judgment.

Hands often express as much as a face. Include them in the portrait when the subject is known to talk with his or her hands.

LDG Productions

Some subjects "talk with their hands," and portraits that include the hands of such people can be particularly expressive.

If your subject wears glasses (as is often the case with older adults), don't make him or her feel awkward by taking them off. You can use the trick mentioned on page 48, or you can use the bounce-flash technique to keep light from reflecting off glasses, and get a picture that truly "reflects" your subject!

This brings up the matter of photographing older adults. Older adults present problems when flaws that often come with age, such as wrinkled skin and double chins, require much more attention in preparation.

To diminish double chins, tell your subject to pretend there is an invisible string attached to the top of his or her head, pulling upward. Tilt his or her face up and then experiment with the position of your light source until you can see the double chin diminished through your viewfinder.

Wrinkles can be dealt with by using either diffused or strong direct light. Diffused light will soften the effect of wrinkles, and strong light directed straight onto your subject's face will erase the wrinkled texture or other flaws of the skin by washing out detail.

The lighting in this photograph softens the image and gives skin tones a beautiful luminescence. The photographer used a telephoto lens to minimize the background and create a close, intimate feeling while maintaining enough distance for the couple to feel at ease.

Don't move in very close to your subject unless you are trying to emphasize character or age. The closer you get to your subject's face, the closer you are to flaws in features and skin texture. You cannot guarantee your subject a flattering picture when you photograph up close.

Remember—especially when you are photographing elderly subjects—to make them comfortable. Don't suggest poses that they won't be able to hold. Their discomfort will be obvious in your photos.

CHILDREN

Children, particularly ones we love, make ideal photographic subjects. Their innocence and honesty of expression can't help but show on film, and their playfulness frequently offers opportunities for great pictures.

Tim Bieber, Inc.

Children have spontaneous expressions that are a joy to capture. These little girls greet the photographer with a mixture of bashfulness and delight. The neutral background helps to accentuate the brightness of their clothing.

Kneeling or sitting gets you on the proper level for photographing a child. Cliché or not, it really is true that the best photographs of a child are usually taken from the child's own level. If you shoot down on a child, the resulting photo may give the impression of an authoritarian adult standing over the child, while shooting upward makes a child look as if he or she were playing adult.

A 50 mm lens was used to photograph this young boy at his own level for a natural perspective. To capture a candid feeling, the photographer waited for the boy to look away from the camera.

Melchior DiGiacomo

If you want shots of children that are totally unposed and candid, you can take pictures from a distance with a telephoto or zoom lens. The distance and the way in which a telephoto lens compresses perspective diminish the difference in height between photographer and subject. A zoom lens allows you to zoom in to catch the expression on one child's face, and then to adjust the lens quickly to show the entire group.

A good way of getting an expressive yet candid shot of a child is to involve him or her in an activity. The boy in the photograph above is so involved in what he is doing that he has lost interest in the camera. At the left, a telephoto lens lets the photographer get right into the center of the action. The child's tension and concentration as he winds up to pitch make an exciting image. Telephoto lenses also throw the background out of focus to help isolate the subject.

Making photography fun for the child almost always guarantees great pictures. Many professionals loosen up a group of children by initiating and then joining in a game. Once the children get involved, the photographer quietly slips away and begins taking pictures.

Encourage your subjects to dress up for the pictures, or to do whatever makes the picture-taking a pleasant, or even exciting, experience. Make up a game, or encourage them to play-act or pose.

About the worst thing you can do is to force children into a very formal situation with many commands such as "do this," "don't do that," or "be sure not to move." Their tension and rigidity will be obvious in your photographs.

Don Klumpp

The children in this photograph are so involved in getting the dog into the treehouse that they seem unaware of having their picture taken. Moments like these make children such rewarding photographic subjects.

Most of all, have confidence in what you are doing. If you are nervous or act unsure, children will pick up on this and become uncomfortable. Don't fidget with your equipment, and don't spend an inordinate amount of time considering and setting up the situation. Even if you are not entirely sure about your equipment, the lighting, or the setting, start shooting before your subject becomes bored, worried, or nervous. Then go with the flow. Rely on your instincts as the situation develops; the poses you want will probably fall into place.

Eric L. Wheater

An awareness of the camera doesn't have to be a bad thing. Most children love having their picture taken, and a little mugging for the camera can create a memorable experience for both of you.

BABIES

Very few photographic subjects are more appealing than infants, babies, and toddlers. The newborn coming home from the hospital, the infant in the bath, the toddler taking first steps—all provide great photographic opportunities.

Every moment in a baby's life can seem like a perfect photo opportunity, but be careful of harsh light that can irritate an infant's eyes. This photograph of a little girl sleeping was taken with plenty of sunlight streaming in from a nearby window. The white linens reflect enough light onto her face to fill shadow areas.

Photography offers a perfect way to record a picture story of our children growing up and to preserve it for the future. Since babies and toddlers change very rapidly from one day to the next, the family album is an important, almost priceless treasure.

Shooting photos for the family album is easy because, in many ways, babies are the perfect models. They have none of the inhibitions and self-consciousness many of us develop as we grow older, and their curiosity and wide-eyed looks make you want to capture their priceless expressions.

Be careful when you move in close to a baby—your camera can be so interesting to a baby that keeping the infant's fingers off the lens might become a problem!

When you photograph infants and babies, soft, natural light—from a large window, or outdoors in shade—usually works best, because it shows their features distinctly, yet smoothly. The light from a flash unit or a single bright bulb can be too harsh to be flattering. It can also irritate an infant and produce expressions of discomfort.

When photographing children at play, set up your camera ahead of time. Then be ready to capture those priceless moments, such as this mischievous exchange between two toddlers.

Bounce flash is a particularly useful technique in photographing babies. It produces soft, even illumination and eliminates the need for direct flash.

To get a happy and bubbly expression from a very young child, work with the parents as they pique the child's interest. In fact, make sure that the parents are always at your side when you photograph an infant. That way, neither the baby nor the parents will be fretful. Besides, infants respond best to their parents, and this can be a big help when you are looking for adorable expressions to photograph.

PHOTOGRAPHING PEOPLE

Babies, more than any other subject, are full of spontaneity and innocence. With a parent standing nearby, the child can often be coaxed into expressions of glee (top) or wonder (bottom). Make sure, however, that you are cautious with your camera equipment when you photograph an infant up close; those little hands and feet move pretty quickly.

Renato de Francesco

G+J Images/W. Steinmetz

PART THREE

CREATING YOUR OWN STYLE

Nancy Brown

What is photographic style? It's more than simply using the proper exposure, focusing correctly, and capturing a good expression—it's also using techniques and materials to produce pictures with a distinctive look and feel.

Experienced amateur and professional photographers know how critical style is in producing successful and effective photographs. Style is a "signature"; it reveals the hand and mind of a photographer—or of any artist, for that matter. Without style, a photograph might as well have been taken by a bank security camera.

Style is hard to define because it is extremely personal. It's the way you see the world, the way you think—it's what you consider important enough to record on film

In Part Three, we will discuss two types of photographic style—candid and formal—which can be quite broad in their application. We will also introduce the technique of soft focus, which some photographers use to create a particular look or feel in their photographs.

CANDID

Some of the most popular photographs of people are pictures that provide a quick glimpse of a person acting naturally, involved in a familiar activity. In these *candid* photos, the subject seems to be unaware that his or her picture is being taken.

Taking candid photos stems from a common impulse to record life as it really is. The most widely seen examples of the candid style come from news photography. In your own experience they may be pictures of people with cake on their noses at a party, or two teams straining to win a tug-of-war at the company picnic.

You may find it easier to take candid shots of people you don't know, such as people you see when you go on vacation. But the candid style can also help you take striking pictures of family and friends, and will impart a feeling of reality or truth that many posed pictures just do not have.

The photographs on these two pages illustrate candid style. At left, the photographer made the shot before the subject became aware of him. The couple below were aware of the camera, but went back to their project, leaving the photographer freedom to snap away.

The first key to a candid photograph is your subject's eyes. If he or she is looking at the camera, people will think that the camera influenced the subject's pose.

Compare two pictures of the same person: one that shows the subject looking at the camera and another that shows the subject looking outside the frame. You'll see that the pictures convey two different moods.

PHOTOGRAPHING PEOPLE

The people in the photograph at the right were so preoccupied that they may have forgotten the photographer entirely. Below, the advantage of distance allowed the recording of this special moment.

Eric Schweikardt

Richard Ustinich

It's hard to be posed and formal when you're jumping into the water! One aspect of candid photography is capturing the zest of the moment.

When you are taking candid pictures, it is important to do so without being obvious. Try to have your camera set for the general lighting conditions and your focus for the approximate distance to your subject. You can pretend to be taking a picture of something else while you watch your real subject out of the corner of your eye. Then, at the proper instant, you can turn to take your picture while the subject is either unaware of or used to your presence.

In fact, if your candid subjects notice you are taking pictures, tell them not to be influenced by the camera. Act confident and friendly. *Keep* taking pictures; your subjects will probably go back to doing what they were doing.

PHOTOGRAPHING PEOPLE

Here, a young man couldn't contain his excitement over winning a trophy. This photograph illustrates that you can take candid pictures even with direct eye contact. Any photograph that captures a personal triumph such as this is a memorable treasure.

Elyse Lewin

Undoubtedly the most useful pieces of equipment in candid photography are telephoto and zoom lenses. With these, you can photograph from a distance without intruding on the subject. At the same time, you will create a feeling of intimacy in your photos, although you may have been nowhere near your subject.

If you do not have a telephoto or zoom lens and you want to take photographs from close up, wait for your subjects to look away from the camera and resume what they were doing.

Never take pictures of people who do not want their pictures taken! It's easy when you're in that "candid portrayal of life" mood to think you have a license to take any photo you want. But, beware: photographing people against their will can lead to arguments and even legal trouble. What's more, in some parts of the world, this behavior transcends mere rudeness and can land you in big, big trouble indeed!

This candid photograph of a baseball team was taken with a long (300 mm) telephoto lens. The long lens allowed the photograher to shoot from a distance without intruding on the team.

Let's restate some handy tips for taking candid pictures:

TO TAKE CANDID PHOTOGRAPHS

- Have your camera set and ready for the situation. Don't waste time—and miss the best picture—by fumbling with your equipment.
- Encourage your subjects to continue doing what they were doing. Ask them to act naturally, and not be influenced by the camera.
- Show confidence in yourself and how the pictures will turn out—it will put your subjects at ease.
- If you have a telephoto or zoom lens, use it! Use the longest focal length you can to photograph from as far away as possible.

FORMAL

Formal refers only to the fact that the subject is obviously posed and is aware of the camera. It does not necessarily mean that a subject is dressed or posed in a particular way.

Formal portraiture provides business for thousands of professional photographers. You don't, however, have to be a professional or own elaborate camera equipment to take formal portraits. With a little practice, your photos can have that "professional" look.

Posing subjects for formal portraits. In almost all formal portraiture, the subject looks directly at the camera, with a relaxed expression or a smile.

As we discussed in the section on photographing adults, study your subject's facial features carefully to determine the best angle from which to photograph. Remember that too much of an angle will show a large nose prominently, and too small an angle will cause large ears to stick out! Chins and necks are also important to watch. Ask your subject to lift his or her chin slightly, or change your camera height slightly, to diminish folds or a double chin. (See page 53 for more specific tips.) But make sure the subject's eyes look open—it is a natural reflex for eyelids to droop when the head is tilted back.

This studio portrait of a young mother and daughter illustrates how fresh and natural a formal portrait can look. As is usually the case, both subjects are looking directly at the camera.

Nancy Brown

As in all photography, framing is important to portraiture. Note how framing this couple horizontally (above) takes in more of their surroundings, while moving closer and framing them vertically (left) eliminates the background and concentrates on their relationship to each other.

PHOTOGRAPHING PEOPLE

David Vance

Keep in mind that photographing a person directly from the front often "flattens out" the subject. A face turned slightly to the side (but with the eyes still facing the camera) usually has a more three-dimensional quality than one photographed straight on. Also, if you place the subject's face and body at a slight angle to the camera, you'll get a more interesting and appealing pose.

Try shooting from various angles to heighten your pictures' dramatic effect. Profiles and three-quarter views are likely to bring fresh interest to your portraits.

Keep props simple. The point of a formal portrait is to show the person in a structured environment. Too much clutter will detract from your subject.

Provide your subject with something to sit on or lean against—poses are likely to be much more interesting. Being forced to stand at attention at a particular spot is enough to make anyone feel—and look—stiff.

Shooting a portrait in profile makes a very dramatic statement. In the photograph above, the man's eyeglasses and fountain pen serve as props; in the photograph on the left, the woman's elaborate hairstyle and gold accents tell us something about her.

You can take formal portraits indoors or out; the use of different backgrounds will enrich your portraits. Indoors, framing your subject in a doorway adds another dimension to your photograph. When you pose your subject outdoors in relatively bright light, depth of field will usually be great enough for both your subject and the background to be in focus. If the background is distracting, change to a larger lens aperture (and faster shutter speed) to produce shallow depth of field. This blurs the background, and creates a soft colorful effect with foliage, brickwork, etc.

A large lens aperture will blur the background and isolate your subject, while a fast shutter speed freezes motion. The combined effect created this simple portrait of a woman on a bicycle.

John P. Kelly

When you shoot outdoor portraits, place your subject in light from the open sky or in a shady area rather than in direct sunlight. Sunlight should not be so harsh that the subject squints or feels uncomfortable. If you do shoot a portrait in bright sunlight, have the subject turn so that the sun hits him or her

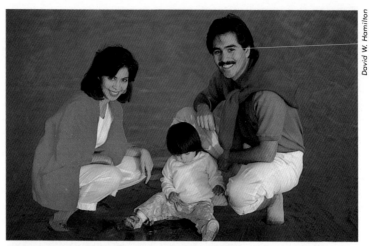

When taking portraits outdoors, make sure that the sun doesn't make your subjects uncomfortable. This photograph of a young family was taken when the sun was at a low (and more flattering) angle. The neutral color of the beach brings out the vibrant colors of their clothing.

from the side, or even from behind. (See the discussion of *backlighting* and *fill-in flash* on pages 16 and 33.)

When you take formal portraits indoors, you can set up the simple studio described on page 48, or simply use whatever comes to hand. With only a large window, a detachable electronic flash, or even a bright household lamp and a reflector, you can produce very flattering effects.

In one of the most common lighting setups for studio portraits, the light strikes the subject at about a 45-degree angle to the front, and slightly above or below eye level. This angle shows the form and texture of the face, and produces just the right reflections in the eyes.

Lighting angles will heighten the drama of your photographs. Sidelighting casts part of your subject in shadow, and gives the portrait dramatic contrasts. You can control and soften the shadows produced by sidelighting by using a reflector to fill the shadows, or by diffusing the light source (see page 22).

PHOTOGRAPHING PEOPLE

You can spread and diffuse light from an electronic flash by using the *bounce-flash technique*. If you have a manual flash unit, you may have to do some calculations or run exposure tests to determine the proper exposure (see the section on bounce flash, page 32).

For other lighting angles, see *frontlighting* on page 50, and backlighting on page 16.

Another special effect that will give your portraits dramatic impact is *soft focus.*

Soft focus envelops your subject in a dreamy haze. You don't get that soft-focus effect you see in many romantic photographs by incorrectly focusing the lens: the photographs are in focus, but they are softened by a diffusion filter.

Soft-focus filters—called *soft, diffusion,* or *fog* filters—are available from a number of manufacturers. Fog filters provide a great deal of diffusion, and are used for landscapes more than for people. Soft filters come in various strengths; a No. 1 filter is the weakest and most commonly used for portraits.

Sidelighting heightens the dramatic impact of a portrait, as in this photograph of a young man. The position of his arms, direct eye contact, and deep shadow on his face make a strong statement.

Daniel Hummel

Light diffused by a thin window curtain and a diffusion filter enhanced the soft, romantic look of this photograph.

You can easily make your own diffusion filter. Simply spread a thin layer of petroleum jelly on a clear skylight (UV) filter. Then check the degree of diffusion by holding the filter up to your eye or attach it to your lens. You can also use hair spray or any number of other substances. Coating a filter with petroleum jelly or clear nail polish provides a reusable diffuser.

Be sure to do this only with filters! Never put anything directly on your lens! You probably won't damage your filters by experimenting with different materials, and even if you do have an accident, the loss will be relatively inexpensive. Damaging a lens, on the other hand, can be very expensive.

Professional photographers who make their own diffusion filters often leave a clear area in the middle if they want to keep the center of the photograph sharp while diffusing the edges. It's up to you, and the effect you are trying to achieve. The list of effects you can produce is endless.

This portrait of a young ballerina is enhanced by strong, warm lighting and a diffusion filter. The effect is contemplative and almost magical.

CONCLUSION. *Photographing People* has presented many techniques for lighting and posing your subjects, as well as tips for developing a style that's distinctly yours.

Now you're ready for the best part. Take what you have learned about lighting and camera angles, films and photographic situations, and use that knowledge in your own photography.

Take things slowly; try to master one technique at a time. Find out which techniques are appropriate to your subjects. When the pictures come out the way you want them to, you'll know the application is a success!

GLOSSARY OF TERMS

Angle of view—The extent of the area "seen" by a lens.

Aperture—The opening in a lens system through which light passes. The size is either fixed or adjustable. Lens openings are expressed as *f*-numbers.

Autofocus—Used to describe cameras that focus automatically on the subject when you aim the camera so that the subject is within the autofocus marks or brackets in the viewfinder.

Automatic flash unit—A flash unit with a sensor that measures the light reflected from a scene or the light at the film plane and shuts off when the proper amount of light has been emitted.

Backlighting—Light shining on the subject from the direction opposite the camera.

Bounce flash—A technique in which flash is directed to (or "bounced" off) a large reflective surface to provide softer, more diffused illumination.

Bounce lighting—Bouncing light from a flash unit or a photolamp off the ceiling or wall to produce a more even, natural effect.

Bracketing—Making extra photographs at exposure settings to provide more and less exposure than the calculated, or recommended setting—for example, at $+1, +2, -1$, and -2 stops from the calculated setting.

Built-in flash unit—A non-detachable unit that is a part of some camera models. It is usually turned on by a button, but some units will automatically activate when the meter determines that the scene is too dark for proper exposure without flash.

Candid pictures—Unposed pictures of people, often taken without the subject's knowledge.

Color balance—The ability of a film to reproduce the colors of a scene accurately. Color films are balanced during manufacture for exposure to light of a certain color quality: daylight, tungsten, etc.

Color temperature—A measurement of the color quality of light sources; expressed in degrees Kelvin (K).

Composition—The arrangement of all elements in a picture: main subject, foreground, background, and supporting subjects.

Contrast—The range of densities in a photograph; the brightness range of a subject or the lighting in a scene.

Conversion filters—Filters used to balance film to a light source different from the source for which it is designed.

Daylight-balanced film—Film that has been balanced to produce accurate color rendition in daylight or with electronic flash.

Dedicated flash—An advanced automatic flash unit designed to work with a specific brand or model of camera. It exchanges information with the camera to set the proper exposure.

Depth of field—The distance between the nearest and farthest objects in a scene that appear in acceptable focus in a photograph. It is determined by the focal length of the lens, the size of the lens opening, and the subject distance. The longer the lens, the larger the opening, or the closer the focus, the shallower the depth of field.

Diffusion—Softening of detail in a photograph by using a diffusion filter or other material that scatters light.

Diffusion filter—A type of filter that diffuses light. Diffusion filters come in varying strengths.

Direct flash—Flash that strikes the subject directly.

Electronic flash—A brief but intense burst of light from the flashtube of a built-in or detachable flash unit; used to supplement existing light or provide the main light on the subject.

Existing light—In photography, existing light is the light that is already on the scene, and includes light from room lamps, fluorescent lamps, spotlights, neon signs, candles, daylight coming through windows, twilight, and moonlight.

Exposure—The amount of light that acts on a photographic material; a product of the intensity (controlled by the lens opening) and the duration (controlled by the shutter speed) of light striking the film or paper.

Exposure meter—An instrument—either built into a camera or a separate, hand-held unit—that measures the intensity of light; used to determine the aperture and shutter speed for proper exposure.

Fill-in flash—Light from a flash unit that is used to brighten shadows created by the primary light source.

Film speed—The sensitivity of a film to light, indicated by a number, such as ISO 200; the higher the number, the more sensitive, or faster, the film.

Film-speed setting—A camera setting—either manual or automatic—that tells the camera the speed of the film.

Filter—A piece of colored glass or other transparent material used over the lens to emphasize, eliminate, or change the color or density of the entire scene or certain elements in the scene.

Flash calculator dial—A control on a flash unit that tells the correct aperture for the camera-to-subject distance, or the correct distance range for a particular aperture.

Flash-synchronization (sync) shutter speed—The speed at which the camera shutter is synchronized with the firing of the flash.

Flashtube—A gas-filled tube that emits a short, intense burst of artificial light.

***f*-number or *f*-stop**—A number used to indicate the size of the opening 'on most cameras lenses. Common *f*-numbers are *f*/2, *f*/2.8, *f*/4, *f*/5.6, *f*/8, *f*/11, *f*/16, and *f*/22. The higher the *f*-number, the smaller the lens opening.

Focal length—The distance from the optical center of a lens to the film plane when the lens is focused at infinity.

Fog filter—See "**Diffusion filter.**"

Formal pictures—Posed pictures of people, taken with the subject's knowledge and often employing direct eye contact.

Frontlighting—Light that strikes the subject from the front.

Hot shoe—The fitting on the camera that holds a portable flash unit. It provides electrical contact with the base of the flash unit so that the flash fires when you press the shutter release.

ISO speed—A system of the International Organization for Standardization for measuring film speed.

Lens—One or more pieces of optical glass or similar material designed to collect and focus rays of light to form a sharp image on the film or paper.

Lens aperture—see "**Aperture.**"

Manual exposure control—A camera exposure system that allows the photographer to adjust aperture and shutter speed manually.

Manual flash—A flash unit that emits the same amount of light each time it fires. It has no sensor to measure and adjust the amount of light.

Normal lens—A lens that produces an image with perspective similar to that of the original scene. A normal lens has a longer focal length and narrower field of view than a wide-angle lens, and a shorter focal length and wider angle of view than a telephoto lens.

Off-camera flash—Using a flash unit off the camera to provide sidelighting, bounce lighting, or other indirect illumination.

Overexposure—A situation in which too much light reaches the film, producing a dense negative or a light slide.

Photolamp—A lamp designed for use in photography that has a color temperature of 3400 K.

Point-and-shoot camera—An automatic non-SLR camera, usually with built-in flash.

Rangefinder—A focusing device on non-SLR cameras. It shows the photographer two images of the subject that must be aligned for proper focus.

Red-eye—A phenomenon caused by reflection of the flash by blood vessels in the back of the eye.

Reflector—Any device used to reflect light onto a subject.

Reflected-light meter—An exposure meter used to measure the amount of light reflecting from a subject.

Sidelighting—Light striking the subject from the side relative to the position of the camera.

Skylight (UV) filter—Used to cut through haze and the blue cast often seen in scenics or photographs made in open shade.

Single-lens-reflex (SLR) cameras—A camera that uses a prism and mirror to provide viewing through the picture-taking lens.

Soft filter—See "**Soft focus.**"

Soft focus—Produced by use of a special filter to soften an image.

Stop(s)—Exposure settings are measured in "stops." Each single-increment change in shutter speed or aperture represents one stop, and halves or doubles the amount of light striking the film. (Also see "***f*-stop.**")

Stop motion—A technique that makes an object in motion appear "stopped"; can be accomplished by using a high shutter speed or electronic flash.

Sync (synchronization) cord—An extension cord that connects the camera to a flash unit to provide electrical contact and synchronization with the shutter.

Telephoto lens—A lens that creates a larger image of the subject than a normal lens at the same camera-to-subject distance.

Three-quarters lighting—Light striking the subject at a 45-degree angle from the line between the subject and the camera.

Through-the-lens meter (TTL)—A built-in camera meter that determines exposure by reading the light passing through the lens.

Tungsten-balanced film—Film that has been balanced to produce accurate color rendition under tungsten light.

Tungsten lamp—A lamp with a color temperature of 3200 K.

Tungsten light—Light from normal household lamps and ceiling fixtures (not fluorescent).

Underexposure—A condition in which too little light reaches the film, producing a thin negative or a dark slide.

Viewfinder—A camera viewing device that shows the subject area that will be recorded on the film.

Wide-angle lens—A lens that covers a wider field of view than a normal lens at the same subject distance.

Zoom lens—A variable-focal-length lens that can be used in place of a number of individual fixed-focal-length lenses.

GLOSSARY

INDEX

Please note: Entries which appear in bold refer to captions.